Magafan (John) v. U.S. Immigration and Naturalization Service U.S. Supreme Court Transcript of Record with Supporting Pleadings

ELMER FRIED, ERWIN N GRISWOLD

Magafan (John) v. U.S. Immigration and Naturalization Service
Petition / ELMER FRIED / 1970 / 1658 / 403 U.S. 931 / 91 S.Ct. 2253 / 29 L.Ed.2d 709 / 4-30-1971
Magafan (John) v. U.S. Immigration and Naturalization Service
Brief in Opposition (P) / ERWIN N GRISWOLD / 1970 / 1658 / 403 U.S. 931 / 91 S.Ct. 2253 / 29 L.Ed.2d 709 / 6-3-1971

Magafan (John) v. U.S. Immigration and Naturalization Service U.S. Supreme Court Transcript of Record with Supporting Pleadings

Table of Contents

SUPREME COURT OF THE UNITED STATES

October Term, 1970

No. 1 �7 � 8

JOHN MAGAFAN,

Petitioner,

-against-

IMMIGRATION & NATURALIZATION SERVICE,

Respondent.

PETITION FOR WRIT OF CERTIORARI TO THE UNITED STATES COURT OF APPEALS FOR THE DISTRICT OF COLUMBIA CIRCUIT

ELMER FRIED
Attorney for Petitioner
515 Madison Avenue
New York, New York
Telephone: (212) 688-8555

Solicitor General
Attorney for Respondent
Department of Justice
Washington, D.C. 20530

THE DICK BAILEY PRINTING SERVICE   Telephone: (212) 447-5358

INDEX

i

REGULATIONS CITED:

Code of Federal Regulations (CFR):

MISCELLANEOUS REFERENCES

SUPREME COURT OF THE UNITED STATES

October Term, 1970

No.

JOHN MAGAFAN,

Petitioner,

v.

IMMIGRATION AND NATURALIZATION SERVICE,

Respondent.

PETITION FOR WRIT OF CERTIORARI

Petitioner prays that a Writ of Certiorari issue to review the order of the United States Court of Appeals for the District of Columbia Circuit, entered in the above cause on February 3, 1971, and the order of said Court denying the petition for rehearing, entered March 1, 1971.

OPINION BELOW

FIRST: The judgment of the United States Court of Appeals for the District of Columbia Circuit is contained in the Appendix, as is the order of said Court denying rehearing. The opinion written by the Board of Immigration Appeals, and the opinion of the Special Inquiry Officer are also contained in the Appendix.

SECOND: The order sought to be reviewed was entered on September 10, 1969, by a Special Inquiry Officer of the Immigration & Naturalization Service, and was affirmed by the Board of Immigration Appeals on May 12, 1971.

This decision was · affirmed by the Court of Appeals on February 3, 1971; order denying petition for rehearing was entered March 1, 1971.

Jurisdiction to review in the matter sought herein is conferred upon this court by 28 U.S.C. Sec. 1254(1).

THIRD: Questions presented for review are as follows:

A. Whether an alien, in transit without visa, who was inspected and admitted into the United States, can adjust his status to permanent residence pursuant to Section 245 of the Immigration & Nationality Act, 8 U.S.C. 1255.

B. Whether a Special Inquiry Officer or the Board of Immigration Appeals has jurisdiction or authority to waive possession of a Visitor's Visa nunc pro tunc.

FOURTH: The statutory sections which the case involves are as follows: Immigration and Nationality Act, 66 Stat. 163 (1952), as amended: Section 214 (a), 8 U.S.C. 1184 (a); Section 238 (d), 8 U.S.C. 1228; Section 245, 8 U.S.C. 1255; Section 248, 8 U.S.C. 1258. The Regulations involved are as follows: Code of Federal Regulations: 8 C.F.R. 212.1 (i); 8 C.F.R. 214.2 (c)(l); 8 C.F.R. 245.1.

STATEMENT OF THE CASE

FIFTH: The order of the Special Inquiry Officer denied the petitioner's application for adjustment of status under Section 245 of the Immigration and Nationality Act, 8 U.S.C. 1255, not as a matter of discretion, but as a matter of law, holding him ineligible because he had been admitted to the United States in transit without a visa. Another portion of the order held the Special Inquiry Officer, and the Board of Immigration Appeals to be without jurisdiction of petitioner's application for nunc pro tunc waiver of a visitor's visa, which waiver, if granted, would have eliminated the basis for petitioner's claimed ineligibility for adjustment of status. The decision of the Special Inquiry Officer was upheld by the Board of Immigration Appeals and by the U.S. Court of Appeals for the District of Columbia Circuit.

The decision with respect to eligibility under Section 245, 8 U.S.C. 1255, was based on 8 C.F.R. 214.2(c)(l), which states that:

> "The privilege of transit without a visa may be authorized only under the conditions that the alien ... will not apply for adjustment of status under Section 245 of the Act..."

and the basis for the denial of the petitioner's application for nunc pro tunc waiver of a visitor's visa was 8 C.F.R. 212.1(i), which states:

> "All district directors ... and all officers in charge of Service Offices outside the United States are authorized to act upon recommendations made by U.S. Consular Officers or by officers of the Visa Office, Department of State, pursuant to the provisions of 22 C.F.R. 41.7 for waiver of visa and passport requirements, under the provisions of Section 212(d)(4)(a) of the Act ..."

The petitioner's basic contentions are as follows: (a) that the Court erred in its interpretation of 8 C.F.R. 214.2(c)(l) so as to bar eligibility for consideration of an adjustment of status application, (b) that if the Court has correctly interpreted that regulation, then the regulation is void as an attempt to abridge a right conferred by statute, and (c) that the Special Inquiry Officer and the Board have jurisdiction to waive, nunc pro tunc, the visa requirements for petitioner's admission to the United States as a temporary visitor under Section 101(a)(15)(B) of the Act, 8 U.S.C. 1101(a)(15)(B), and thus had jurisdiction to cure the ineligibility which the Board found by virtue of 8 C.F.R. 214.2(c)(1).

John Magafan is the only non-citizen member of a family well-established in the United States. He arrived in New York from Greece on October 20, 1968. He was not in possession of a visa, nor did he need one, since his purpose in entering the United States was to transfer to a connecting flight to Miami, Florida, where he was scheduled to meet the ship S/S Diana, which would take him out of the country—a common situation in which a passenger is admitted in transit (Section 101(a)(15)(C) of the Act, 8 U.S.C. 1101(a)(15)(C)) under a waiver of nonimmigrant visa (Section 212(d)(4)(C) of the Act, 8 U.S.C. 1182(d)(4)(C)).

The airplane was late in arriving in New York, and as a result, he missed his connecting flight. Upon arrival, Mr. Magafan was inspected, his passport withheld, and he was told to proceed to the Olympic Airlines Office to arrange an alternate connecting flight. His American brothers were at the Airport, and they told Mr. Magafan that his mother was severely ill. Overwhelmed by concern and remorse, he left the Airlines Office and rushed to his mother's side.

On January 20, 1969, Mr. Magafan filed an application with the District Director of the Immigration & Naturalization Service at Baltimore, Maryland, for adjustment of status under Section 245 of the Immigration & Nationality Act, 8 U.S.C. 1255. It was summarily rejected, and his application fee was returned. The denial was based on 8 C.F.R. 214.2(c)(1). A

4

deportation proceeding was commenced, and a hearing accorded him on September 10, 1969, during which he renewed his application for adjustment of status, as authorized in 8 C.F.R. 242.17. The Special Inquiry Officer denied the application, relying on the Board of Immigration Appeals decision in *Matter of Davis,* 10 I&N Dec. 441. Mr.Magafan then appealed to the Board of Immigration Appeals which affirmed the Special Inquiry Officer's decision, refusing to reconsider *Matter of Davis.*

The decision of the Board of Immigration Appeals was then appealed to the U.S. Court of Appeals for the District of Columbia Circuit. The Court of Appeals affirmed the decision of the Board of Immigration Appeals, citing the opinion of the 2nd Circuit in *Fook Hong Mak v. Immigration and Naturalization Service,* 435 F.2d 728 (2d Cir. 1970).

BASIS FOR FEDERAL JURISDICTION

SIXTH: The federal statute which formed the basis for the deportation proceeding was the Immigration and Nationality Act, 66 Stat. 163 (1952), as amended, 8 U.S.C. 1101, *et. seq.,.* Jurisdiction was vested in the U.S. Court of Appeals for the District of Columbia Circuit by virtue 8 U.S.C. 1105a.

REASONS FOR ALLOWING THE WRIT

SEVENTH:

A. *The issues presented by the instant petition are of great significance and should be determined by this Court.*

Thousands of aliens enter the United States each year in transit without visa. These persons are denied the opportunity to apply for adjustment of status through the action of the Immigration and Naturalization Service, which the Court of

5

Appeals has sanctioned. Aliens in transit who desire to become permanent resident aliens and who are eligible for permanent resident status under the Immigration Selection System are forced to depart from the United States and receive immigrant visas abroad, frequently causing personal hardship and needless expense to the individual. Yet, the statute grants to these aliens, as well as numerous other classes of aliens, the right to apply for adjustment of status while in the United States.

The right to apply for adjustment of status in the United States is a valuable right (between 25,000 and 30,000 aliens adjust their status under Section 245, 8 U.S.C. 1255 each year) which has been conferred by Congress. Only Congress possesses the authority to revoke or deny that right.

Moreover, the issues raised in this petition go to the very essence of government—the interrelation between the executive branch and the legislative branch. The Court of Appeals failed to differentiate between a broad grant of discretionary power to an administrative agency by the legislature and a narrow grant of discretionary power. The significance of this distinction extends far beyond the subject of immigration law to all matters where the Congress has empowered an administrative agency to administer a law. The decision below, unreversed, will virtually emasculate the legislature in those areas where the legislature desires to rigidly control the meaning of a statute. The decision below would allow an administrative agency to substitute its judgment for that of the elected representatives of the people. In relying upon the opinion of the Court of Appeals of the Second Circuit in *Fook Hong Mak v. Immigration and Naturalization Service, supra*, the Court of Appeals has rendered a decision which would allow the most circumscribed delegation of authority to be interpreted as the delegation of broad discretionary authority. The proper balance between the legislative and executive branches of government can only be maintained by the courts carefully and studiously weighing the

6

degree of discretionary authority which Congress intended to delegate. Only through consideration by this Court can the legislative prerogative be restored.

Finally, in relying upon the decision of the Court of Appeals for the Second Circuit, the Court of Appeals failed to deal with significant issues raised by the instant case but not considered in *Fook Hong Mak v. Immigration and Naturalization Service, supra.*

B. *Section 245 of the Immigration and Nationality Act, 8 U.S.C. 1255, permits an alien entering the United States in transit without visa, to apply for adjustment of his status to that of a permanent resident.*

Section 245(a) permits any alien (other than a crewman) who was inspected, and admitted, or paroled into the United States, to apply for adjustment of his status to that of a permanent resident. Section 245(c) exludes from this privilege aliens who are natives of the Western Hemisphere. Thus, the Section makes clear that there are only three classes of aliens who are not eligible to adjust status under Section 245: (1) aliens who are not inspected and admitted, or paroled into the United States (in short, those who made clandestine entries and evaded inspection altogether), (2) aliens who, although inspected, had the status of crewmen (a class of aliens who had created special enforcement problems for the Immigration & Naturalization Service), and (3) natives of the Western Hemisphere (as to whom special problems had also caused Congress to bar them from this relief).

Aliens, such as the Petitioner herein, who were admitted in transit, whether with or without a waiver of the visa requirement, but who were inspected and admitted, are not mentioned by Congress as one of the barred classes. Since statutes should be interpreted as they normally read, transits

7

were intended by Congress to be eligible to adjust status under Section 245. Indeed, the Government at no point argues that Section 245 can be read as barring this petitioner from eligibility. The government instead argues that a *regulation*, 8 C.F.R. 214.2(c)(1) bars petitioner's eligibility.

In *Fook Hong Mak v. Immigration and Naturalization Service, supra,* the court found that this regulation did not exceed statutory authority, but was merely a manifestation of the exercise of discretionary power by the Attorney General, and further, that broad discretionary authority had been delegated to him. We submit that this conclusion was erroneous.

The history of the statutory evolution and development of Section 245 of the Immigration and Naturalization Act and related Sections clearly demonstrates an exercise of tight control by Congress over the detailed policies and provisions of this Section. Congress carefully set forth the classes of persons not eligible for adjustment of status. There was no intention on behalf of Congress to relinquish authority to the Immigration and Naturalization Service. Congress chose not to delegate broad discretionary power. However, the Immigration and Naturalization Service has attempted to usurp this power by promulgating regulations in excess of their delegated authority.

Regulations in excess of Congressional authority and in violation of a statute will not stand. *Gutknecht v. U.S. 396 U.S. 295 (1969).*

Congress formulated the language of Section 245 on four different occasions. Its initial phraseology, in 1952 (66 Stat. 163) (Legislative History in 2 U.S. Cong. News (1952) pp. 1718-1719), limited the privilege to aliens who had: (a) been lawfully admitted as nonimmigrants and (b) who, at the time of applying, had been maintaining their lawful nonimmigrant status. In that form of phraseology, alien crewmen were eligible

8

under Section 245, and so were natives of the Western Hemisphere. Only natives of adjacent islands and contiguous territory were barred.

In 1958, the Section was liberalized, by allowing aliens who, after a lawful nonimmigrant entry, had violated status and had ceased to maintain their nonimmigrant status, to adjust status. (72 Stat. 699) (Legislative History at 2 U.S. Cong. News (1958), pp. 3698-3699)). In 1960, to deal with an increasingly vexing problem of deserting crewmen, and, at the request of the Immigration & Naturalization Service, Congress amended the law to bar alien crewmen from eligibility to adjust status (74 Stat. 504). In 1965, to deal with the problem created by the increasing number of South Americans who were coming to the United States with tourist visas, and then promptly applying to adjust status under Section 245, Congress further limited Section 245 by making ineligible natives of the Western Hemisphere with the exception of refugees from Western Hemisphere countries (79 Stat. 918).

In connection with the 1960 amendment, the House Committee on the Judiciary said (2 U.S. Cong. News (1960) pp. 3147)):

> "under the proposed amendment to Section 245(a) the procedure for the adjustment of the immigration status of aliens to that of aliens lawfully admitted for permanent residence would be broadened so as to include all aliens (other than alien crewmen) who have been inspected and admitted, or who have been paroled into the United States, thereby providing considerably more flexibility in the administration of the law".

During the same time period, Congress manifested a desire to treat aliens in transit similarly to crewmen in some respects and dissimilarly in other respects. In section 248 of the Act, 8

U.S.C. 1258, Congress enacted a provision for change of status from one nonimmigrant classification to another nonimmigrant classification; just as in Section 245, Congress expressly excluded certain classes of aliens from eligibility.

The following categories of non-immigrants are not entitled to the benefits of Section 248: an alien classified as a crewman (8 U.S.C. 1101(a)(15)(D)), a transit (8 U.S.C. 1101(a)(15)(C)) or an exchange visitor (8 U.S.C. 1101(a)(15)(J)). There is an exception that a transit or an exchange visitor can apply to become a non-immigrant under 8 U.S.C. 1101(a)(15)(G). However, the exceptions do not apply to the crewmen.

Similarly, in Section 238(d) of the Act, 8 U.S.C. 1228(d), Congress explicitly barred from eligibility under Section 248, those aliens who were admitted in immediate and continuous transit through the United States destined to foreign countries.

Prior to April, 1969, the Committee on the Judiciary of the House of Representatives had a provision within their internal rules of procedure (Rule 6) which barred aliens who are crewmen, stowaways, or transit from an automatic stay of deportation during the pendancy of the private bill once reports have been requested. In April, 1969, students, exchange visitors and visitors were added to the category of aliens to whom this provision applied. In February 1971, the provision was extended to all nonimmigrant categories.

The Committee on the Judiciary of the House of Representatives favorably reported a bill on June 4, 1968, which was subsequently defeated on the floor of the House. This bill, H.R. 15651, 90th Congress, 2d Sess. (1968) would have facilitated the entry into the United States of foreign tourists for a period of 90 days. A provision set forth in the bill would have prohibited adjustment of status under Section 245 of any person entering the U.S. pursuant to its provisions.

This brief summary of Congressional activity with regard to transits clearly shows that Congress intended to designate the manner in which transits would be treated under the Immigration and Nationality Act. *The detailed policies were decided by Congress, not delegated to the Attorney General.* Thus, to conclude that the general language of Section 214 (a), 8 U.S.C. 1184 (a) and Section 103(a), 8 U.S.C. 1103(a) authorizing the Attorney General to prescribe conditions in the admission of aliens, constitutes a broad grant of discretionary power is to disregard the entire context of the Act. In the face of Congress' demonstrated ability to write explicit language to bar transits of all kinds (with and without visas) from eligibility to adjust to nonimmigrant status under Section 248, it is absurd to find that Congress was so poverty stricken in language as to be unable to write the same restrictions into Section 245—if Congress had intended to bar transits under Section 245.

There are various types of standards. Professor Davis has observed:

> A standard, principle or rule can be so vague as to be meaningless, it can have a slight meaning or considerable meaning, it can have some degree of controlling effect, or it can be so clear and compelling as to leave little or no room for discretion. Davis, *Discretionary Justice: A Preliminary Inquiry* (1969)

The standard contained in the Act for the restriction upon various non-immigrant categories is of the last type. When Professor Davis speaks about confining and refining broad grants of discretion, he refers to the first two types.

The portions of Professor Davis' book cited in *Fook Hong Mak* decision specifically refer to situations in which there has been too broad a delegation of discretionary power and a need to confine the broad discretion through agency action. No one could maintain that excessive discretionary authority has been delegated to the Attorney General with regard to transits or, for that matter, other non-immigrant categories within the Immigration and Naturalization Act.

The court in *Fook Hong Mak*, at 731, rejects the argument that because two exceptions are set forth in Section 245, Congress intended to prevent the designation of any other class or similar treatment, which would limit the Attorney General to the exercise of discretion solely on a case-by-case basis. However, the Court fails to distinguish between aliens in transit without visas which have been closely scrutinized by Congress, and all other groups. The broader question of whether any group could have potentialities or actualities of abuse so similar to those manifest by the two classes designated in Section 245 that promulgation of a regulation barring such persons from adjustment of status would be within the ambit of the Attorney General's power is not in issue. With regard to *transits*, Congress has ably displayed a knowledge of potential and actual abuses of various descriptions and has chosen to place numerous restrictions upon transits. If Congress had found that transits had abused the privileges accorded them as they found the crewmen had abused the privileges, Congress would merely have placed transits in Section 245.

In the treatment of transits, Congress clearly does not need "legislative assistance" from the Immigration & Naturalization Service. Congress expressed its judgment as to the restrictions upon classes which it considered in depth. There can be no doubt that transits were considered in depth.

At 731, the Court in *Fook Hong Mak* sets forth at length a justification for the action of the Attorney General in prohibiting aliens in transit from adjusting status. Whether or not such conclusions by the Attorney General would have been justified is unimportant. Congress considered elements similar

12

to those postulated by the Court in enacting legislation, which renders various categories of aliens ineligible for the benefits of Section 245, and which excludes transits from eligibility for change from one nonimmigrant status to another under Section 248. See S. Rep. 748, 89th Cong., 1st Sess. at 24 (1965); H. Rep. 745, 89th Cong., 1st Sess. at 22 (1965); S. Rep. 1651, 2 U.S. Cong. News at 1696-7, 1718-19, 1721-2 (1952); H Rep. 1137, 82nd Cong., 2d Sess. at 19-20, 24-26, 35, 36 (1952). Congress, in its wisdom, chose the manner in which aliens in transit should be treated. Neither the Immigration and Naturalization Service nor the Courts should be allowed to alter the explicit intention of Congress.

The Government in this case, does not go so far as to say that Section 245 actually does include an eligibility bar against the petitioner. It finds the bar to exist in the language of 8 C.F.R. 214.2(c)(1) which authorizes the admission of a transit without visa on the condition that the alien not apply for adjustment of status under Section 245. From the fact that the regulation sets up such a condition, the Board of Immigration Appeals draws the legal conclusion that the alien is barred under Section 245. Title 8 of the Code of Federal Regulations is keyed to the equivalent sections of the Statute. Had the regulations actually intended to bar transits without visas from eligibility under Section 245, the regulations would presumably have been written articulately enough to have stated so specifically; such language would have been found in 8 C.F.R. 245.1. Although 8 C.F.R. 245.1 specifically enumerates a list of persons not eligible to adjust status under Section 245, not a single word is to be found in this regulation which purports to bar transits with or without visas. 8 C.F.R. 245.1, under the title "Eligibility", lists the following ineligibles: (1) Aliens who arrived as crewmen; (2) aliens who were not admitted, or paroled following inspection by an immigration officer; (3) natives of any country of the Western Hemisphere, or of an adjacent island; (4) refugees unless also qualified under a different provision of law: (5) exchange aliens, unless

13

compliance with the foreign residence requirements have been complied with or waived; (6) foreign government officials and treaty aliens unless they have filed a waiver of privileges inherent in their status; (7) immediate relatives or preference aliens unless they are the beneficiaries of valid unexpired visa petitions: (8) non-preference aliens who are not exempted from Labor Certification requirements unless a Labor certification has been issued, or the alien is within one of the excepted classes.

Part 245 of the Regulations contains no reference to the ineligibility of transits without visas.

Yet, the Government can only point to 8 C.F.R. 214.2(c)(1), as its justification for the inference that a transit without a visa is not eligible. In the absence of specific language in the regulations creating ineligibility, coupled with the absence in the statute of any language creating ineligibility, there is no basis whatever for the position that a transit without visa is ineligible under Section 245. 8 C.F.R. 214.2(c)(1) states that as a condition of admission the alien in transit without visa will not apply for adjustment of status under Section 245. Interestingly, 8 C.F.R. Section 214 contains no similar provision establishing as a condition of admission that an alien will not apply for adjustment of status. Such a condition of admission is only prescribed for the alien in transit without visa. A transit without visa admitted on condition that he not apply, violates a condition of his admittion if he does apply. The penalty for that violation is the transit privilege, which might be a very valuable privilege to him, can then be withdrawn and the alien deported from the United States. It is not only transits without visas who are admitted on condition. 8 C.F.R. 214.1(a) sets up conditions for the admission of "every known immigrant alien applicant for admission". One of the conditions is that *every* such applicant —

"...agree that he will abide by all the terms and conditions of his admission..."

Yet, the Board of Immigration Appeals has never held that an alien visitor, or student, or treaty-trader, etc., *who violates a condition of admission* is thereby precluded from applying under Section 245.

All that the regulation (8 C.F.R. 214.2(c)(1)) does is set up an *additional* condition for the admission of transits without visas, the additional condition being an implied agreement that he will not apply to adjust status under Section 245. But, his violation of that condition cannot have any greater effect of his statutory right under Section 245, than the violation by him, or by any non-immigrant alien, of any of the other numerous conditions of admission. We submit that the regulation can be read consistently with the statute, and be upheld only by interpreting it as meaning that an alien admitted in transit without a visa, who files an application to adjust status under Section 245, may have his transit privilege terminated, and be subject to deportation proceedings by virtue of his filing that application.

The application for adjustment of status should still be considered on its merits. As a matter of discretion, the Attorney General may take into account the violation of the condition of admission, just as he presently considers failure to comply with the conditions of admission in the case of a visitor or student unlawfully working or many other such situations. He may deem such a violation sufficient to deny the application for permanent residence. Whether or not he could deny applications filed by all transits as a class under the theory that this would be an appropriate exercise of discretion is not the point in this case. The Immigration and Naturalization Service did not accept jurisdiction and adjudicate the petitioner's application and then deny the requested relief. The Immigration

15

and Naturalization Service summarily rejected the application, returning it and the required filing fee. Even if all applications for adjustment of status submitted by transits were accepted and then denied on the ground that this constituted an exercise of discretion toward a class, such action would constitute an abuse of discretion. It is very clear that there might well be applicants, who entered as transits without visas, whose equities are much more urgent and compelling than the cases of aliens who enter as students or as tourists. The Attorney General is not exercising discretion when he arbitrarily establishes categories of persons who are barred, regardless of the merits of their particular cases. See 2 Gordon & Rosenfield, *Immigration Law & Procedure*, Section 8.15, Pages 8-298, citing *James v. Shaughnessy*, 202 F.2d 519 (2nd Cir. 1953), cert. denied 345 U.S. 969; *McGrath v. Khristensen*, 340 U.S. 162 (1950); *Brownell v. Gutnayer*, 94 U.S.App. D.C. 90. 212 F.2d 462 (1954); *Dessalernos v. Savoretti*, 356 U.S. 269 (1958); *Tibke v. U.S. Immigration & Naturalization Service*, 335 F.2d 42 (2d Cir. 1964). See, *Fong v. Brownell*, 215 F.2d 683 (1954).

The decision of the Second Circuit in *Fook Hong Mak* fails to distinguish between a regulation which establishes ineligibility for adjustment of status and a regulation which prescribes a condition for admission into the United States. In fact, the decision fails to raise the issue. The regulation is treated as though it were an enumerated category under the Regulations for Section 245 and, consequently, a ground of ineligibility for the benefits of Section 245.

The Attorney General originally requested that Congress place the category of crewmen within Section 245 of the Act, thus, barring their eligibility to apply for adjustment of status. The Attorney General did not, at that time, take it upon himself to either place crewmen within the regulations under Section 245 of classes for whom adjustment of status would be barred, nor did he go to Congress and request that aliens in

16

transit without visa be placed within the explicit categories of persons barred from adjustment of status within the Immigration and Nationality Act. If both classes do, in fact, present. similar patterns of abuse which justify similar treatment, it is indeed interesting that they are not handled in the same way under the law. Section 214 prescribes conditions of admission. If the Attorney General sought to bar eligibility rather than establish a condition of admission, it is indeed peculiar that he placed the category transits within the regulations to Section 214 and not within the designated classes encompassed within the regulations under Section 245. The Attorney General should not now be permitted to interpret the regulations in a manner inconsistent with the language of the regulation. In the instant case, the regulations have been applied as though aliens in transit without visa were ineligible for the benefits of adjustment of status. It has not been interpreted as a condition of admission. In ignoring this distinction, the Attorney General is seeking to do indirectly what he did not do directly.

It is a basic principle of law that a statutory right may only be relinquished *voluntarily*, and there cannot be a voluntary relinquishment unless the right is known to exist, and the alien intends to relinquish it. There is no evidence on the record that this alien was ever advised that he might have a right under Section 245, at the time he landed in the United States; and certainly, no evidence that he was told that by accepting the transit privilege, he would be voluntarily waiving that right; and finally, from the known conditions prevailing at airports of entry, with their enormous workloads, and lack of interpretive facilities, one may assume that no attempt was made to obtain a voluntary relinquishment. It is certainly true that if ineligibility under Section 245 is to depend upon the concept of voluntary relinquishment in exchange for the transit privilege, there would have to be a specific finding with a knowing and intentional waiver of the Section 245 right. *(Bachman v. United States*, 327

17

F.2d 415 (9th Cir. 1964); *In Re Baud*, 299 F. Supp. 565 (DC W.Va. 1969). In the instant case, there has been no such finding.

C. *The Special Inquiry Officer and the Board of Immigration Appeals had authority to waive possession of a visitor's visa and to have admitted petitioner in that status nunc pro tunc.*

The petitioner's request for a nunc pro tunc waiver of a visitor's visa was an attempt to obtain a status which would have made him eligible for adjustment of that status under Section 245, 8 U.S.C. 1255. If this request had been granted, and he had been deemed admitted as a visitor (as distinguished from his actual status as transit without visa), no question of his eligibility to adjust status under Section 245 would remain. The denial of this request was not made in the exercise of discretion, but was predicated solely upon a lack of jurisdiction, or power to consider the request. The Board, in affirming the Special Inquiry Officer's renunciation of authority, cited no precedent. The view was taken that only District Directors of the Immigration & Naturalization had this power pursuant to 8 C.F.R. 212.1 (i). Wholly inconsistent with this abdication of authority, however, is the Board's decision in the *Matter of Estrada-Morena*, 11 I & N Decision 249, in which the Board held that the passport requirement of Section 212 (a) (20), 8 U.S.C. 1182 (a) (20), of the Immigration & Nationality Act was properly waived nunc pro tunc by the Special Inquiry Officer in deportation proceedings. 8 C.F.R. 212.1 (i) delegates to District Directors the power to waive both visa requirements and passport requirements. It is simply not consistent for the Board to hold that the delegation to District Directors in that regulation did not bar the Special Inquiry Officer from waiving the passport requirement and, yet, did bar the Special Inquiry Officer from waiving the visa requirement. If a Special Inquiry Officer can waive one, he necessarily has jurisdiction to waive the other; if he has no jurisdiction to waive one, he cannot have jurisdiction to waive the other.

8 C.F.R. 242.17 (d) states:

"Nothing contained herein is intended to foreclose the respondent from applying for any benefit, or privilege, which he believes himself eligible to receive in proceedings under this part."

If this regulation constitutes a grant of power to enable a hearing official to grant an application to waive a passport, perforce it constitutes a grant of power to waive a visa. The Special Inquiry Officers, and the Board of Immigration Appeals have never held themselves powerless in exclusion proceedings to waive possession of a visa (Matter of Millard, 11 I & N Dec. 175; Matter of Riva, All 239 287). There is no basis in any statute or regulation which grants them more power in the one situation than in the other.

Additionally, the Board of Immigration Appeals and, in fact, Special Inquiry Officers have virtually all the powers of the Attorney General in passing on cases within their jurisdiction (1 Gordon & Rosenfield, *Immigration Law and Procedure*, Section 1.10 (c); 8 C.F.R. 3.1 (d) (1)). The power of the District Director to grant the waiver is merely a delegation of power from the Commissioner of Immigration & Naturalization, who in turn derived his authority from the Attorney General by delegation. The Board of Immigration Appeals. deriving its power directly from the Attorney General, has at least coordinate, or concurrent powers with District Directors, so that whichever delegatee has the case before him has the authority to decide it. It is therefore correct that District Directors have authority to grant passport and visa waivers in cases pending before them; but it is equally correct that the Board of Immigration Appeals has at least equal authority in cases pending before it.

Had the Special Inquiry Officer and had the Board considered the equities of the situation, the waiver might well have been granted. We will never know how discretion would have been exercised, since there was no attempt to exercise it. This Court should remand the proceeding with directions to the Board of Immigration Appeals to exercise its authority. If the authority is exercised in favor of the alien, he would then be eligible to adjust status under Section 245, even if transits without visas were held not to be eligible.

The decision below ought not be permitted to stand, for it denies a right conferred by statute upon a class of persons; unreversed, it threatens the structure of the democratic system by ceding a major portion of the function of the legislative branch to the executive branch of government.

Respectfully submitted,

Elmer Fried

Attorney for Petitioner
515 Madison Avenue
New York, New York 10022

Solicitor General
Attorney for Respondent
Department of Justice
Washington, D.C. 20530

JUDGEMENT OF THE COURT OF APPEALS

UNITED STATES COURT OF APPEALS
For the District of Columbia Circuit

[no opinion]

No. 24,350   September Term, 1970

JOHN MAGAFAN, Petitioner   United States Court of Appeals
for the District of Columbia Circuit

v.

FILED FEB 1971

U.S. Immigration and
Naturalization Service,
Respondent

Nathan J. Paulson
CLERK

Petition for Review of an Order of the Board of Immigration Appeals.

Before: WRIGHT and McGOWAN, Circuit Judges, and GIGNOUX,* United States District Judge for the District of Maine.

JUDGMENT

This case came on to be heard on the record on appeal from the Board of Immigration Appeals, and was argued by counsel. While the issues presented occasion no need for an opinion, they have been accorded full consideration by the court. *See* Local Rule 13(c).

On consideration of the foregoing, it is ORDERED and ADJUDGED by this court that the order of the Board of Immigration Appeals appealed from in this cause is hereby affirmed. *See Fook Hong Mak v. Immigration and*

Naturalization Service, 2 Cir.. ⎯⎯ F.2d ⎯⎯ (Docket No. 34237, decided November 24, 1970).

PER CURIAM

Dated: February 3, 1971

⎯⎯⎯⎯⎯⎯⎯⎯⎯⎯

*Sitting by designation pursuant to 28 U.S.C. § 292(c) (1964)

ORDER DENYING MOTION FOR REHEARING

UNITED STATES COURT OF APPEALS
For the District of Columbia Circuit

⎯⎯⎯⎯⎯⎯⎯⎯

No. 24,350   September Term, 1970

John Magafan, Petitioner   United States Court of Appeals
                             for the District of Columbia Circuit

v.

                             FILED MAR 1 1971
U.S. Immigration and
Naturalization Service,   Nathan J. Paulson
Respondent   CLERK

Before: Wright and McGowan Circuit Judges; Gignuox
U.S. District Judge for the District of Maine.

A2

ORDER

On consideration of petitioner's petition for rehearing, it is

ORDERED by the Court that petitioner's aforesaid petition is denied.

Per Curiam

For the Court:

NATHAN J. PAULSON
Clerk

*U.S. District Judge Gighoux sitting by designation pursuant to Title 28 U.S. Code Section 292(c).

OPINION OF THE BOARD OF IMMIGRATION APPEALS

UNITED STATES DEPARTMENT OF JUSTICE
BOARD OF IMMIGRATION APPEALS

File: A18 730 921 - Baltimore
In re: JOHN IOANNIS MAGAFAN

IN DEPORTATION PROCEEDINGS
APPEAL

ORAL ARGUMENT: January 13, 1970
    On behalf of respondent: Elmer Fried, Esquire
                                515 Madison Avenue
                                New York, New York 10022

    On behalf of I& N Service: Irving A. Appleman
                                Appellate Trial Attorney

A3

OPINION

The respondent, a native and citizen of Greece, has been found deportable under the provisions of section 241(a)(2) of the Immigration and Nationality Act, in that, after admission as a transit without visa, he has remained in the United States for a longer time than permitted. He appeals from an order entered by special inquiry officer on September 10, 1969 granting him the privilege of voluntary departure in lieu of deportation with an alternate order of deportation in the event he fails to depart when and as required. Exceptions have been taken to the finding of deportability (p. 3).

The respondent, a married male alien, 44 years of age, last entered the United States through the port of New York on or about October 20, 1968. He was admitted as a transit without visa and authorized to remain in the United States until October 21, 1968 (Ex. 5). He has remained in the United States subsequent to October 21, 1968 without authority and is deportable as charged in the Order to Show Cause.

There is evidence of record that the respondent filed an

A4

application for an adjustment of status under section 245 of the Act with the District Director at Baltimore. Maryland on January 20, 1969 (Ex. 4). The application was rejected by the District Director on April 18, 1969 on the ground that the respondent was precluded from applying for adjustment of status by the provisions of 8 C.F.R. 214.2(c)(1) (Exs. 2 and 3). The application for adjustment of status was again renewed during the hearing accorded the respondent on September 10, 1969 (pp. 9 and 10). The special inquiry officer denied the application relying on this Board's decision in *Matter of Davis*, 10 I&N Dec. 441 (BIA 1964). We held in *Matter of Davis* (supra) that an alien who enters the United States as a transit without visa is. precluded from adjusting his status by the provisions of 8 C.F.R. 214.2(c)(1).*1/*

Counsel maintains that our decision in *Matter of Davis* should be overruled. Counsel argues that this Board errs in failing to distinguish between a condition of admission as set forth in 8 C.F.R. 214.2(c)(1) and eligibility under section 245. He reasons that every nonimmigrant alien enters under certain conditions and makes implicit promises without being barred from eligibility under section 245. He points to the fact that a nonimmigrant tourist is admitted under the condition that he will depart when his visit or any extension thereof ends, or when he abandons his authorized nonimmigrant status (8 C.F.R. 214.1(a). It is counsel's position that if a breach of promise by a tourist, that he will depart, does not result in ineligibility, why should the breach of promise by a transit

---

1/ 8 C.F.R. 214.2(c)(1) reads in pertinent part: "The privilege of transit without a visa may be authorized only under the conditions . . . that the alien will not apply for extension of temporary stay or for adjustment of status under section 245 of the Act . . ."

without visa, that he will not apply under section 245, result in ineligibility?

We reject the argument advanced by counsel in support of his position. Section 245 of the Act provides the Attorney General with the discretion to adjust the status of an alien nonimmigrant, other than an alien crewman and a native of the Western Hemisphere including adjacent islands, "under such regulations as he may prescribe." The Attorney General, pursuant to this authority, has promulgated a regulation which in effect precludes a non-immigrant transit without visa from establishing his eligibility for adjustment of status under section 245 of the Act because he cannot apply for the benefits thereof (8 C.F.R. 214.2(c)(1)). The regulation has the force and effect of law. Furthermore, section 214(a) of the Act specifically provides "The admission to the United States of any alien as a non-immigrant shall be for such time and under such conditions as the Attorney General may by regulations prescribe." (Emphasis supplied.) Under the statute the Attorney General has ample authority to authorize the entry of a nonimmigrant transit without visa on the condition that the transit alien will not apply for adjustment of status under section 245 of the Act.

The argument advanced by counsel in this proceeding was before the court in *Tomasello v. Rogers*, 306 F. Supp. 705 (S.D.N.Y. 1969). The court held (306 F.Supp. at 711):

The Attorney General . . . in his discretion, pursuant to specific statutory authority to regulate the admission of aliens as non-immigrants . . . has conditioned the grant of this privilege so that aliens accorded transit without visa status are precluded from applying for adjustment of their status. Having accepted the benefits of transit without visa status, the (alien) is now bound by the applicable conditions.

OPINION

The respondent during the course of the hearing moved for a waiver of nonimmigrant visa requirements pursuant to section 212(d)(3) of the Immigration and Nationality Act and the nunc pro tunc admission of the respondent as a visitor for pleasure under section 101(a)(15)(D) of the Act (p. 13).

OPINION OF THE SPECIAL INQUIRY OFFICER

UNITED STATES DEPARTMENT OF JUSTICE
IMMIGRATION AND NATURALIZATION SERVICE

File: A18 730 921 - Baltimore, Maryland

In the Matter of

JOHN (IOANNIS) MAGAFAN

                              IN DEPORTATION PROCEEDINGS
Respondent

CHARGE: I & N Act - Section 241(a)(2), TRWOV, remained longer

APPLICATION: Termination of proceedings; adjustment under Section 245; waiver of visa; nunc pro tunc change of status from TRWOV to visitor without visa; in the alternative, voluntary departure.

IN BEHALF OF RESPONDENT: IN BEHALF OF SERVICE:

Elmer Fried, Esquire   Newton T. Jones
515 Madison Avenue   Trial Attorney
New York, New York 10022   Philadelphia, Pa.

A7

OPINION

ORAL DECISION OF THE SPECIAL INQUIRY OFFICER
ENTERED SEPTEMBER 10, 1969

The respondent is a 44-year-old married male, native and citizen of Greece, who entered the United States at New York, New York, on or about October 20, 1968, and was admitted as a transit without visa. He was authorized to remain in the United States until October 21, 1968, and this is evidenced by exhibit 5 in the record. He has remained in the United States after October 21, 1968, without authority of the Immigration and Naturalization Service. The order to show cause was amended in allegations 4 and 5, so that the dates in those allegations, October 30, were amended to read October 21. This amendment was made at the hearing. I find that deportability in the case has been established. Deportability has not been conceded by counsel. Counsel's contention is that an application for adjustment of status under Section 245, which had been submitted to the District Director, and was rejected by the District Director, should have been adjudicated by the District Director and that if that had, in fact, occurred the respondent would not now be in an unlawful status. The heart of the issue in this case is the question whether a person admitted as a transit without visa is eligible for adjustment of status under Section 245. Respondent, through counsel, has made a number of motions and requests, including a motion to terminate proceedings. He has submitted an application for adjustment of status under Section 245; he has submitted an application for a waiver of visa and for a nunc pro tunc change of status from transit without visa; he has urged that the respondent be considered as having been paroled into the United States. The contentions of counsel may have merit; one or more of these contentions may have merit, but at this time I am bound by the interim decision of the Board of Immigration Appeals in *Matter of Davis*, 10 I & N 441. In effect, should I

A8

accept any of counsel's contentions, I would be overruling this
interim decision. This I do not have the power to do. It is
possible that counsel may be able to persuade the Board of
Immigration Appeals that it should overrule *Matter of Davis.*
The Board, of course, has the power to overrule its own prior
decision. I do not. I will therefore not discuss in detail the
various motions made by counsel. They are set forth fully in the
record and I am sure counsel will urge them effectively upon
appeal. In the alternative, respondent has requested the privilege
of voluntary departure. He has established eligibility under the
statute and the regulations for that relief and I will grant it as a
matter of administrative discretion. I note that the respondent
has his parents, two brothers and two sister, all of whom are
United States citizens and all of whom are residing in the
United States. His wife is here as a visitor. There are no relatives
outside the United States. I am entering an order at this time,
therefore, denying adjustment of status under Section 245; all
the concomitant motions and requests made by counsel in
connection with that request for adjustment under Section 245
are also denied.

ORDER: It is ordered that in lieu of an order of deportation
the respondent be granted voluntary departure, without
expense to the Government, on or before October 10, 1969, or
any extension beyond that date that may be granted by the
District Director and under such conditions that the District
Director shall direct.

IT IS FURTHER ORDERED that if the respondent fails to
depart when and as required the privilege of voluntary
departure shall be withdrawn without further notice or
proceedings and the following order shall thereupon become
immediately effective: the respondent shall be deported from
the United States to Greece on the charge contained in the

order to show cause.

Herman L. Bookford
Special Inquiry Officer

Opinion of U.S. Court of Appeals
For the Second Circuit

UNITED STATES COURT OF APPEALS
FOR THE SECOND CIRCUIT

————————

No. 163—September Term, 1970.
(Argued October 29, 1970   Decided November 24, 1970)
Docket No. 34237

————————

FOOK HONG MAK,

Petitioner,

-against-

IMMIGRATION AND NATURALIZATION SERVICE,

Respondent.

————————

Before:

MOORE, FRIENDLY and ADAMS,*

Circuit Judges.

————————

Petition to review an order for the deportation of an alien
who had been admitted to the United States in transit without a

* Of the Third Circuit, sitting by designation.

A10

visa, on the ground that the Attorney General unlawfully failed to exercise discretion under Section 245 of the Immigration and Nationality Act to consider whether the alien should be allowed to adjust his status to that of an alien lawfully admitted for permanent residence. Petition denied.

––– ––– ––– ––– –––

STANLEY H. WALLENSTEIN, Assistant United States Attorney (Whitney North Seymour, Jr., United States Attorney for the Southern District of New York, of Counsel), *for Respondent.*

MARTIN H. LEONARD, Esq. (John L. Murff, Esq., New York, New York, of Counsel), *for Petitioner.*

––– ––– ––– ––– –––

FRIENDLY, *Circuit Judge:*

Petitioner Fook Hong Mak, a fifty year old, married male alien, is a citizen of the Republic of China. In April 1968 he was admitted to the United States without a visa, pursuant to Section 101 (a)(15)(C) and Section 214 of the Immigration and Nationality Act of 1952 and the Regulations thereunder, 8 C.F.R. Section 214.2(e)(1), as a nonimmigrant alien "in immediate and continuous transit through the United States." He was on a journey from Hong Kong to South America, in the course of which an eight day lay-over in this country had been authorized. When the INS discovered that he was still here six months later, it began a deportation proceeding. Conceding deportability, Fook Hong Mak sought two forms of discretionary relief — adjustment of status to that of an alien lawfully admitted for permanent residence under Section 245 or, failing that, voluntary departure under Section 244(e).

A11

Section 245, so far as here material, reads as follows:

(a) The status of an alien, other than an alien crewman, who was inspected and admitted or paroled into the United States may be adjusted by the Attorney General, in his discretion and under such regulations as he may prescribe, to that of an alien lawfully admitted for permanent residence if (1) the alien makes an application for such adjustment, (2) the alien is eligible to receive an immigrant visa and is admissible to the United States for permanent residence, and (3) an immigrant visa is available to him at the time his application is approved.

* * * * *

(c) the provisions of this section shall not be applicable to any alien who is a native of any country of the Western Hemisphere or of any adjacent island named in Section 101(b)(5).

Acting under the authority specifically delegated to him by the Immigration and Nationality Act, the Attorney General adopted a regulation, 8 C.F.R. Section 214.2(c), which in its present form [1] provides:

Section 214.2 Special requirements for admission, extension, and maintenance of status.
The general requirements in Section 214.1 are modified for the following nonimmigrant classes:

* * * * *

(c) Transits — (1) Without visas. An applicant for admission under the transit without visa privilege must

1 The applicable provision of the Regulation was first promulgated in 1963. 28 F.R. 3078. The Regulation has since been amended several times with respect to matters not material here.

A12

establish that he is admissible under the immigration laws; that he has confirmed and onward reservations to at least the next country beyond the United States, and that his departure from the United States will be accomplished within ten calendar days after his arrival. . . . The privilege of transit without a visa may be authorized only under the conditions that the carrier, without the prior consent of the Service, will not refund the ticket which was presented to the Service as evidence of the alien's confirmed and onward reservation, *that the alien will not apply for extension of temporary stay or for adjustment of status under Section 245 of the Act*, and that at all times he is not aboard an aircraft which is in flight through the United States he shall be in the custody directed by the district director.[2] (Emphasis supplied.)

Conceding that Fook Hong Mak met the three numbered requirements of Section 245(a) and that the presence in the United States of his wife and children, at least one of whom is a citizen, made even temporary departure somewhat of a hardship, the Board of Immigration Appeals, affirming the Special Inquiry Officer, found that the italicized condition of the Regulation precluded consideration of his application for such relief. It granted the alternative request for voluntary departure, which will enable the petitioner to apply from abroad for entry as an immigrant. Fook Hong Mak says that whether or not the Board would have been justified in denying his application for adjustment of status on the merits, the

2 While the Regulation in question was codified under § 214 in the Code of Federal Regulations, the authority under which it was issued derives not only from §214 of the Act, whereby "[t]he admission to the United States of any alien as a nonimmigrant shall be for such time and under such conditions as the Attorney General may by regulations prescribe," but also from §103, charging the Attorney General with "the administration and enforcement of this chapter and all other laws relating to this chapter" including the establishment of "such regulations . . . as he deems necessary for carrying out his authority," and § 245, providing for the adjustment of status of aliens "in his discretion and under such regulations as he may prescribe."

Attorney General's self-imposed restriction on the consideration of it is unlawful.[3]

We are unable to understand why there should be any general principle forbidding an administrator, vested with discretionary power, to determine by appropriate rule-making that he will not use it in favor of a particular class on a case-by-case basis, if his determination is founded on considerations rationally related to the statute he is administering. The legislature's grant of discretion to accord a privilege does not imply a mandate that this must inevitably be done by examining each case rather than by identifying groups. The administrator also exercises the discretion accorded him when, after appropriate deliberation, he determines certain conduct to be so inimical to the statutory scheme that all persons who have engaged in it shall be ineligible for favorable consideration, regardless of other factors that otherwise might tend in their favor. He has then decided that one element is of such determinative negative force that no possible combination of others could justify an affirmative result. By the same token he could select one characteristic as entitling a group to favorable treatment despite minor variables. Nothing in this offends the basic concept that like cases should be treated similarly and unlike ones differently. The administrator has simply determined that the one paramount element creates such "likeness" that other elements cannot be so legally significant as to warrant a difference in treatment. This may be an even "juster justice" than to accord different treatment because of trivial differences of fact; at least it is competent for the administrator to think so. The leading student of the problem has recently counseled:

3   After the submission of briefs in this case, another panel of this court sustained the validity of the Regulation ina per curiam opinion, *La Franca v. INS*, F.2d (1970), slip opinion 167. In apparent recognition that the brief of counsel for La Franca did not challenge the validity of the Regulation with anything like the force of petitioner's brief here, the INS does not seriously object to our considering the issue on its merits. If we were to disagree with our brothers, which we do not, *in banc* consideration would be required.

A14

When legislative bodies delegate discretionary power without meaningful standards, administrators should develop standards at the earliest feasible time, and then, as circumstances permit, should further confine their own discretion through principles and rules.

Davis, Discretionary Justice: A Preliminary Inquiry 55 (1969).

The authorities cited to us would not lead to any contrary view. *United States ex rel. Accardi* v. *Shaughnessy*, 347 U.S. 260 (1954), rested on the basis that the Attorney General by regulation had delegated discretion to the Board of Immigration Appeals but then had precluded the Board from exercising it in certain instances. Here the Special Inquiry Officer and the Board are empowered to exercise only such discretion as the Attorney General himself could do within the Regulations he has prescribed. In *Mastrapasqua v. Shaughnessy*, 180 F.2d 999, 1002 (2 Cir. 1950), all the judges agreed that the Attorney General could set up a class of cases as to which he would refuse to exercise discretion, provided the class was "rationally differentiated from other cases, not within that class, where he uses his discretion case by case." The difference of opinion was whether the classification there was capricious, as the majority held, or rational, as the dissenting judge thought. We have stated more recently, in *U. S. ex rel. Stellas v. Esperdy*, 366 F.2d 266, 269-70 (2 Cir. 1966), vacated and remanded at the INS' suggestion, on a point not here material, 388 U.S. 462 (1967):

. . . the Attorney General may govern the exercise of his discretion by written or unwritten rules; indeed it would be remarkable if he did not. Any such decision is an application of facts to principles. All this regulation does is provide a substitute for the exercise of discretion on a case by case basis. But there has been an exercise of discretion;

A15

. . . We know of no rule which requires a case by case approach; the Attorney General certainly may proceed by regulation.

The Attorney General's determination that aliens who had obtained admission without a visa as being "in immediate and continuous transit through the United States," Section 101(a)(15)(C), should not be eligible to apply for adjustment of status under Section 245 was reasonably related to the statutory scheme. Both the definition and other provisions of the Immigration and Nationality Act, notably Section 238(d) which authorizes the Attorney General to enter into contracts with transportation lines guaranteeing that such passage will occur, show that Congress authorized the Attorney General to accord the unusual benefit of admission as a nonimmigrant and without a visa only because quick departure was assured. It was reasonable for the Attorney General to conclude that aliens admitted on so fleeting a basis were not within the spirit of Section 245 and thus could not deserve favorable exercise of his discretion, even if they came within the letter. He could properly have thought also that to entertain such applications in any case would encourage aliens to obtain admission under the pretense that they were in "immediate and continuous transit" and then stay on for years, as Fook Hong Mak has managed to do,[4] thereby upsetting the balance of benefit and burden that Congress had envisioned. He could have thought further that affording such encouragement might create such burdens for transportation lines that had contracted to assure the departure of such aliens as to make them reluctant to do so and in the long run thus impede the facility of international travel which the privilege of transit without visa was intended to enhance.

4   The time involved in appeals from discretionary denials on the part of the Special Inquiry Officer to the Board of Immigration Appeals, and from the Board's affirmance to a court of appeals, is also relevant.

A16

Petitioner argues that however the matter might otherwise stand, the Attorney General's blanket exclusion of transits without visas from consideration for status adjustment under Section 245 was unauthorized because that section itself states two exceptions – alien crewmen and aliens who are natives of any country of the Western Hemisphere or any adjacent island named in Section 101(b)(5). But it is fallacious to reason that because Congress *prevented* the Attorney General from exercising any discretion in favor of those groups, which Congress had found to have abused the privileges accorded them,[5] it meant to *require* him to exercise it in favor of everyone else on a case-by-case basis even if experience should convince him of the existence of another group with similar potentialities or actualities of abuse.[6] Cf. *Pfizer, Inc. v. Richardson*, —— F.2d ——, —— (2 Cir. 1970), slip opinions 265, 283. Having expressed its judgment that two categories should be ineligible for the exercise of discretion, Congress left it open to the Attorney General to determine whether the applications of all other aliens seeking status adjustment under Section 245 should be evaluated on the merits of each case or whether some categories were susceptible to handling on a less individualized basis. See Davis, *supra*, at 56.

The petition to review is denied.

---

5   See House Report No. 2088, 86th Cong. 2d Sess., p. 2 (1960); Sen. Rep. No. 748, 89th Cong. 1st Sess., p. 24 (1965).

6   This also disposes of appellant's contention that the last sentence in § 238(d), "[n]otwithstanding any other provision of this chapter, such aliens may not have their classification changed under section 248 . . .," is indicative of a congressional intent to require case-by-case disposition of all applications for status adjustment under §245.

A17

RELEVANT STATUTES AND REGULATIONS

ADMISSION OF NONIMMIGRANTS

(a) Section 214 (a), 8 U.S.C. 1183(a). The admission to the United States of any alien as a nonimmigrant shall be for such time and under such conditions as the Attorney General may by regulations prescribe, including when he deems necessary the giving of a bond with sufficient surety in such sum and containing such conditions as the Attorney General shall prescribe, to insure that at the expiration of such time or upon failure to maintain the status under which he was admitted, or to maintain any status subsequently acquired under section 248, such alien will depart from the United States.

ENTRY THROUGH OR FROM FOREIGN CONTIGUOUS TERRITORY AND ADJACENT ISLANDS; LANDING STATIONS

Section 238(d), 8 U.S.C. 1255:

"(d) The Attorney General shall have power to enter into contracts including bonding agreements with transportation lines to guarantee the passage through the United States in immediate and continuous transit of aliens destined to foreign countries. Notwithstanding any other provision of this Act, such aliens may not have their classification changed under section 248.

ADJUSTMENT OF STATUS OF NONIMMIGRANT TO THAT OF PERSON ADMITTED FOR PERMANENT RESIDENCE; RECORD; NATIVES OF CONTIGUOUS COUNTRY OR ADJACENT ISLAND

Section 245, 8 U.S.C. 1255:

"(a) The status of an alien, other than an alien crewman, who was inspected and admitted or paroled into the United

States may be adjusted by the Attorney General, in his discretion and under such regulations as he may prescribe, to that of an alien lawfully admitted for permanent residence if (1) the alien makes an application for such adjustment, (2) the alien is eligible to receive an immigrant visa and is admissible to the United States for permanent residence, and (3) an immigrant visa is immediately available to him at the time his application is approved."

* * * * * * * * * *

"(c) The provisions of this Section shall not be applicable to any alien who is a native of any country of the Western Hemisphere or of any adjacent island named in section 101 (b) (5)."

CHANGE OF NONIMMIGRANT CLASSIFICATION

Section 248, 8 U.S.C. 1258:

"The Attorney General may, under such conditions as he may prescribe, authorize a change from any non-immigrant classification to any other nonimmigrant classification in the case of any alien lawfully admitted to the United States as a nonimmigrant who is continuing to maintain that status, except an alien classified as a nonimmigrant under paragraph (15)(d) of section 101(a), or an alien classified as a nonimmigrant under paragraph (15)(c) or (J) of section 101(a) unless he applies to have his classification changed from a classification under paragraph (15)(C) or (J) to a classification under paragraph (15)(A) or (15)(G) of section 101(a)."

8 C.F.R. 212.1(i)

"All district directors. . .and all officers in charge of Service

Offices outside the United States are authorized to act upon recommendations made by U.S. Consular Officers or by officers of the Visa Office, Department of State, pursuant to the provisions of 22 C.F.R. 41.7 for waiver of visa and passport requirements, under the provisions of Section 212 (d)(4)(a) of the Act..."

8 C.F.R. 214.2(c)(1):

". . .The privilege of transit without visa may be authorized only under the conditions. . .that the alien will not apply for extension of temporary stay or for adjustment of status under section 245 of the Act. . ."

8 CFR – PART 245 – ADJUSTMENT OF STATUS TO THAT OF PERSON ADMITTED FOR PERMANENT RESIDENCE

"245.1 *Eligibility* – (a) *General.* An alien who on arrival in the United States was serving in any capacity on board a vessel or aircraft, or was destined to join a vessel or aircraft in the United States to serve in any capacity thereon, or was not admitted or paroled following inspection by an immigration officer is not eligible for the benefits of section 245 of the Act. An alien who is a native of any country of the Western Hemisphere or of any adjacent island named in Section 101(b)(5) of the Act is not eligible for the benefits of section 245 of the Act. An alien who has been allocated an immigrant visa number and who entered the United States conditionally pursuant to section 203(a)(7) of the Act, is not eligible for the benefits of section 245 of the Act unless he qualifies as an immediate relative pursuant to section 201(b) of the Act on the basis of a visa petition approved in his behalf or as a special immigrant within the meaning of section 101(a)(27) of the Act.

A20

(b) *Exchange aliens.* Pursuant to section 212(e) of the Act, an alien who has or has had the status of an exchange alien or of a nonimmigrant under section 101(a)(15)(J) of the Act is not eligible for the benefits of section 245 of the Act, section 13 of the Act of September 11, 1957, or section 1 of the Act of November 2, 1966, unless he has complied with the foreign-residence requirements of section 212(e) of the Act or has been granted a waiver thereof.

(c) *Officials and treaty aliens.* An alien who has a nonimmigrant status under paragraph (15)(A), (15)(E), or (15)(G) of section 101(a) of the Act, or has an occupational status which would, if he were seeking admission to the United States, entitle him to a nonimmigrant status under any of such paragraphs of section 101(a) of the Act is not eligible for the benefits of section 245 of the Act, section 13 of the Act of September 11, 1957, or section 1 of the Act of November 2, 1966, unless he first executes and submits with his application the written waiver required by section 247(b) of the Act and Part 247 of this chapter. A member of the immediate family of an alien having status under section 101(a)(15)(A) or (G) of the Act, and a spouse or child of an alien having status under section 101(a)(15)(E) of the Act may apply for adjustment of status only if such member, spouse, or child executes the written waiver required by section 247(b) of the Act, irrespective of whether the principal alien also applies for adjustment and executes such waiver.

(d) *Immediate relatives under section 201(b) and preference aliens under section 203(a)(1) through 203(a)(7).* An applicant who claims immediate relative status under section 201(b) or preference status under section 203(a)(1) through 203(a)(6) of the Act is not eligible for the benefits of section 245 of the Act unless he is the beneficiary of a valid unexpired visa petition filed in accordance with Part 204 of this chapter and approved to accord him such status. An alien who claims preference status under the proviso to section 203(a)(7) of the Act is not eligible for the benefits of section 245 of the Act and as provided in Sec. 245.4, unless the district director has approved the alien's Application for Classification as a Refugee under the Proviso to Section 203(a)(7), Immigration and Nationality Act.

(e) *Non-preference aliens.* An applicant who is a nonpreference alien seeking adjustment of status for the purpose of engaging in gainful employment in the United States, and who is not exempted under Sec. 212.8(b) of this chapter from the labor certification requirement of section 212(a)(14) of the Act, is ineligible for the benefits of section 245 of the Act unless an individual labor certification is issued by the Secretary of Labor or his designated representative, or unless the applicant establishes that he is within Schedules A or C —Precertification List, 29 CFR Part 60."

No. 1658

Supreme Court, U.S.
FILED
JUN 3 1971
E. ROBERT SEAVER, CLERK

In the Supreme Court of the United States
OCTOBER TERM, 1970

JOHN MAGAFAN, PETITIONER

v.

IMMIGRATION AND NATURALIZATION SERVICE

*ON PETITION FOR A WRIT OF CERTIORARI TO THE
UNITED STATES COURT OF APPEALS FOR
DISTRICT OF COLUMBIA CIRCUIT*

BRIEF FOR THE UNITED STATES IN OPPOSITION

ERWIN N. GRISWOLD,
  Solicitor General,

WILL WILSON,
  Assistant Attorney General,

BEATRICE ROSENBERG,
CRAIG M. BRADLEY,
  Attorneys,
  Department of Justice,
  Washington, D. C. 20530.

In the Supreme Court of the United States

OCTOBER TERM, 1970

No. 1658

JOHN MAGAFAN, PETITIONER

v.

IMMIGRATION AND NATURALIZATION SERVICE

---

*ON PETITION FOR A WRIT OF CERTIORARI TO THE
UNITED STATES COURT OF APPEALS FOR
DISTRICT OF COLUMBIA CIRCUIT*

BRIEF FOR THE UNITED STATES IN OPPOSITION

OPINION BELOW

The judgment of the court of appeals (Pet. App. A1-A2) was entered without an opinion. The opinion of the Board of Immigration Appeals (Pet. App. A3-A7) is not reported.

JURISDICTION

The judgment of the court of appeals was entered on February 3, 1971. A petition for rehearing was denied on March 1, 1971. On April 30, 1971, the petition for a writ of certiorari was filed. The jurisdiction of this Court is invoked under 28 U.S.C. 1254(1).

(1)

QUESTIONS PRESENTED

1. Whether the Attorney General was authorized by Congress to declare a nonimmigrant alien in transit without visa ineligible for an adjustment of status under Section 245 of the Immigration and Nationality Act.

2. Whether the Special Inquiry Officer had the power to alter petitioner's classification *nunc pro tunc* from transit without visa to nonimmigrant visitor.

STATUTE AND REGULATION INVOLVED

Section 245(a) of the Immigration and Nationality Act (8 U.S.C. 1255(a)) provides that:

> (a) The status of an alien, other than an alien crewman, who was inspected and admitted or paroled into the United States may be adjusted by the Attorney General, in his discretion and under such regulations as he may prescribe, to that of an alien lawfully admitted for permanent residence if (1) the alien makes an application for such adjustment, (2) the alien is eligible to receive an immigrant visa and is admissible to the United States for permanent residence, and (3) an immigrant visa is immediately available to him at the time his application is approved.

8 C.F.R. 214.2 provides in relevant part that:

> The general requirements in § 214.1 are modified for the following nonimmigrant classes:

* * * * *

(c) *Transits*—(1) *Without visas.* An applicant for admission under the transit without visa privilege must establish that he is admissible under the immigration laws; that he has confirmed and onward reservations to at least the next country beyond the United States, and that his departure from the United States will be accomplished within ten calendar days after his arrival * * *. * * * The privilege of transit without a visa may be authorized only under the conditions that the carrier, without the prior consent of the service, will not refund the ticket which was presented to the Service as evidence of the alien's confirmed and onward reservation, that the alien will not apply for extension of temporary stay or for adjustment of status under section 245 of the Act, and that at all times he is not aboard an aircraft which is in flight through the United States he shall be in the custody directed by the district director.

STATEMENT

The essential facts are not in dispute. Petitioner, a Greek national, entered this country on October 20, 1968, as a nonimmigrant alien without a visa in immediate and continuous transit through the United States. Although he had never worked on a ship, he was allegedly en route from Greece to Miami, Florida, where he was to board a Greek vessel as a seaman. He was to remain in this country for one day, until October 21, 1968.

Upon his arrival in New York, petitioner claims that he was met at the airport by his American brothers and told that his mother, who was already in this country, was very ill. His story is that he thus went with his brothers to his mother's side rather than proceeding on to Miami, Florida (Pet. 4).

Some three months later, on January 20, 1969, petitioner sought to obtain an adjustment of status to permanent residence pursuant to Section 245 of the Immigration and Nationality Act, 18 U.S.C. 1255. The District Director rejected the application on the ground that, as a visitor in transit without visa, petitioner was precluded by the terms of 8 C.F.R. 214.2(c)(1)[1] from applying for that form of relief (Pet. App. A5).

On July 2, 1969, petitioner was ordered to show cause why he should not be deported. A hearing was held on September 10, 1969, during which he again applied for an adjustment of status. The Special Inquiry Officer (Pet. App. A7-A10) found him ineligible for such relief but granted him the option of voluntary departure in lieu of deportation. Petitioner then took an appeal to the Board of Immigration Appeals; on May 12, 1970, the Board, relying on its earlier decision in *Matter of Davis*, 10 I & N Dec. 441 (BIA 1964), held that petitioner was not entitled to an adjustment of status (Pet. App. A3-A7). The United States Court of Appeals for the District of Columbia Circuit affirmed *per curiam*

---

[1] The regulation provides in pertinent part as follows: "The privilege of transit without a visa may be authorized only under the conditions * * * that the alien will not apply for extension of temporary stay or for adjustment of status under section 245 of the Act * * *."

(Pet. App. A1-A2), and denied a petition for re-hearing (Pet. App. A2-A3).

ARGUMENT

1. Petitioner concedes that he entered this country as an alien without a visa for "immediate and continuous transit through the United States" under Section 101(a)(15)(C) of the Immigration and Nationality Act, 8 U.S.C. 1101(a)(15)(C), and that he violated a condition of his entry by remaining here beyond the one-day period allotted to him for transit to Miami, Florida. He contends, however, that the summary rejection of his Section 245 application for adjustment of status was unjustified. Specifically, he urges that the regulation barring his application, 8 C.F.R. 214.2(c)(1), relates solely to Section 214 of the Act (8 U.S.C. 1184), which authorizes the Attorney General to prescribe conditions to the admission of any alien, and thus does not foreclose applications for adjustment to permanent residence status under the separate statutory provisions of Section 245. Such an interpretation would, he argues further, be contrary to the intent of Congress, which specifically excluded other classes of aliens from eligibility for Section 245 relief, but did not exclude aliens in transit without a visa.

a. The fact that aliens in transit are barred from applying for adjustment of status by a regulation promulgated under Section 214 of the statute does not thereby make the regulation inapplicable to such aliens seeking permanent residence under Section 245. Section 214(a) (8 U.S.C. 1184(a)) provides:

> The admission to the United States of any alien as nonimmigrant shall be for such time and under such conditions as the Attorney General may by regulations prescribe * * *.

The general rule, as expressed in Section 212(a) (26) of the Act (8 U.S.C. 1182(a)(26)), is that nonimmigrants are excludable unless they possess a visa and passport. Pursuant to Section 212(d)(4) (C) (8 U.S.C. 1182 (d)(4)(C)), however, Congress has authorized the Attorney General and the Secretary of State, acting jointly, to waive the visa and passport requirements in the case of aliens "in immediate and continuous transit through the United States." In exercising this authority, the Attorney General chose to admit such aliens on the condition that they not be eligible to apply for adjustment of status under Section 245. As the Second Circuit recently held in *Fook Hong Mak* v. *Immigration and Naturalization Service*, 435 F.2d 728, 731 (Pet. App. A16), that determination "was reasonably related to the statutory scheme." Having once imposed the condition in 8 C.F.R. 214.2(c)(1), the Attorney General was not required to repeat it in another part of the regulations before it could take effect. See *La Franca* v. *Immigration and Naturalization Service*, 433 F. 2d 992 (C.A. 2); *Tomasello* v. *Rogers*, 306 F. Supp. 705 (S.D. N.Y.).

b. Nor is there any substance to petitioner's contention that this conclusion is contrary to the intent of Congress. The answer to this argument was given by the Second Circuit in *Fook Hong Mak* (Pet. App. A17): " * * * it is fallacious to reason that because Congress *prevented* the Attorney General from exercising any discretion in favor of those groups, which Congress had found to have abused the privileges accorded them, it meant to *require* him to exercise it in favor of everyone else on a case-by-case basis even if experience should convince him of the existence of another group with similar potentialities or actualities of abuse" (emphasis in original; footnotes omitted).[2] To the contrary, Section 245 in specific terms delegates to the "Attorney General, in his discretion and under such regulations as he may prescribe" (8 U.S.C. 1255), explicit authority to treat additional classes of aliens in the same manner that Congress has chosen to treat those groups within the statutory exclusion, if he determines that there are "some categories * * * susceptible to handling on a less individualized basis." *Fook Hong Mak* v. *Immigration and Naturalization Service, supra* (Pet. App. A17). See generally 8 C.F.R. 245.1(a) (alien who has been allocated an immigrant visa number); 8 C.F.R. 245.1(b) (exchange alien); and see *Gambino* v. *Immigration and Naturalization Service,* 419 F. 2d 1355 (C.A. 2), certiorari denied, 399 U.S. 941; *Tuazon* v. *Immigration and Naturalization Service,* 389 F. 2d 363 (C.A. 7). And, as explained in *Fook Hong Mak* (Pet. App. A16), it was not unreasonable for

---

[2] Section 245 specifically excludes two classes of aliens from eligibility for adjustment of status under that provision—alien crewmen and aliens who are natives of any country of the Western Hemisphere or any adjacent island named in Section 101(b)(5), 8 U.S.C. 1101(b)(5).

the Attorney General to conclude that aliens in transit without visa constitute such a category. Thus, for him to declare this group ineligible for Section 245 relief is a valid exercise of his authority.

2. Petitioner's additional contention that the Special Inquiry Officer and the Board of Immigration Appeals had authority to waive possession of a visitor's visa and to admit petitioner as a visitor *nunc pro tunc* is without merit. Section 248 of the Act (8 U.S.C. 1258), which governs changes of non-immigrant classifications, expressly forbids changing the classification of "* * * an alien classified as a nonimmigrant under paragraph 15(C) ["aliens in immediate and continuous transit through the United States"] * * * of section 1101(a) of this title."

CONCLUSION

For the reasons stated, it is respectfully submitted that the petition for a writ of certiorari should be denied.

ERWIN N. GRISWOLD,
Solicitor General.

WILL WILSON,
Assistant Attorney General.

BEATRICE ROSENBERG,
CRAIG M. BRADLEY,
JUNE 1971. *Attorneys.*

☆ U. S. GOVERNMENT PRINTING OFFICE; 1971   426466   607

CPSIA information can be obtained
at www.ICGtesting.com
Printed in the USA
BVHW012029060219
539515BV00054B/810/P

9 781270 510413